The
13 Clocks

Andrew
May, 1995

JAMES THURBER

The
13 Clocks

ILLUSTRATED BY MARC SIMONT

A Yearling Book

Published by
Dell Publishing
a division of
Bantam Doubleday Dell Publishing Group, Inc.
666 Fifth Avenue
New York, New York 10103

The trademark Yearling® is registered in the U.S. Patent and Trademark Office.

The trademark Dell® is registered in the U.S. Patent and Trademark Office.

ISBN: 0-440-40582-3

Reprinted by arrangement with Donald I. Fine, Inc.

Printed in the United States of America

March 1992

10 9 8 7 6 5 4 3 2 1

WES

To Jap and Helen Gude
who have broken more than one spell
cast upon the author by a witch or wizard,
this book is warmly dedicated.

F O R E W O R D

I wrote *The Thirteen Clocks* in Bermuda, where I had gone to finish another book. The shift to this one was an example of escapism and self-indulgence. Unless modern Man wanders down these byways occasionally, I do not see how he can

11

hope to preserve his sanity. I must apologize to my publishers and to the talented Marc Simont, who were forced to keep up with the constant small changes I insisted on making all the time, even in the galley proofs. In the end they took the book away from me, on the ground that it was finished and that I was just having fun tinkering with clocks and running up and down secret stairs. They had me there.

I want to thank these helpful friends:

Sara Linda Williams, for letting me use her name for the Princess (Miss Williams, who is four, insisted on oleanders in the Princess's hair instead of freesias, and there were several grueling conferences about this, from which I barely emerged the winner); John and Nelga Young, who provided the perfect place to write the story; Fritzi Kuegelgen, who was able by some magic of her own to make out and transcribe some five hundred sheets of pencil scrawl and to read the whole thing aloud from beginning to end at least a dozen times; Ronnie and Janey

12

Williams, for brightening the weather by their presence on an island in the ocean seas; and my wife, for constructive criticism and for waking me out of nightmares, some of them about the Todal, I suppose, but the worst ones, on the darkest nights, about the whole enterprise in general.

J. T.

West Cornwall
Connecticut

The 13 Clocks

I

NCE upon a time, in a gloomy castle on a lonely hill, where there were thirteen clocks that wouldn't go, there lived a cold, aggressive Duke, and his niece, the Princess Saralinda. She was warm in every wind and weather, but he was always cold. His hands were as cold as his smile and almost as cold as his heart. He wore gloves when he was asleep, and he wore gloves when he was awake, which made it difficult for him to pick up pins or coins or the kernels of nuts, or to tear the wings from nightingales. He was six feet four, and forty-six, and even colder than he thought he was. One eye

wore a velvet patch; the other glittered through a monocle, which made half his body seem closer to you than the other half. He had lost one eye when he was twelve, for he was fond of peering into nests and lairs in search of birds and animals to maul. One afternoon, a mother shrike had mauled him first. His nights were spent in evil dreams, and his days were given to wicked schemes.

Wickedly scheming, he would limp and cackle through the cold corridors of the castle, planning new impossible feats for the suitors of Saralinda to perform. He did not wish to give her hand in marriage, since her hand was the only warm hand in the castle. Even the hands of his watch and the hands of all the thirteen clocks were frozen. They had all frozen at the same time, on a snowy night, seven years before, and after that it was always ten minutes to five in the castle. Travelers and mariners would look up at the gloomy castle on the lonely hill and say, "Time lies frozen there. It's always Then. It's never Now."

The cold Duke was afraid of Now, for Now has warmth and urgency, and Then is dead and buried. Now might bring a certain knight of gay and shining courage — "But, no!" the cold Duke muttered. "The Prince will break himself against a new and awful labor: a place too high to reach, a thing too far to find, a burden too heavy to lift." The Duke was afraid of Now, but he tampered with the clocks to see if they would go, out of a strange perversity, praying that they wouldn't.

Tinkers and tinkerers and a few wizards who happened by tried to start the clocks with tools or magic words, or by shaking them and cursing, but nothing whirred or ticked. The clocks were dead, and in the end, brooding on it, the Duke decided he had murdered time, slain it with his sword, and wiped his bloody blade upon its beard and left it lying there, bleeding hours and minutes, its springs uncoiled and sprawling, its pendulum disintegrating.

The Duke limped because his legs were of different lengths. The right one had outgrown the left because, when he was young, he had spent his mornings place-kicking pups and punting kittens. He would say to a suitor, "What is the difference in the length of my legs?" and if the youth replied, "Why, one is shorter than the other," the Duke would run him through with the sword he carried in his swordcane and feed him to the geese. The suitor was supposed to say, "Why, one is longer than the other." Many a prince had been run through for naming the

wrong difference. Others had been slain for offenses equally trivial: trampling the Duke's camellias, failing to praise his wines, staring too long at his gloves, gazing too long at his niece. Those who survived his scorn and sword were given incredible labors to perform in order to win his niece's hand, the only warm hand in the castle, where time had frozen to death at ten minutes to five one snowy night. They were told to cut a slice of moon, or change the ocean into wine. They were set to finding things that never were, and building things that could not be. They came and tried and failed and disappeared and never came again. And some, as I have said, were slain, for using names that start with X, or dropping spoons, or wearing rings, or speaking disrespectfully of sin.

The castle and the Duke grew colder, and Saralinda, as a princess will, even in a place where time lies frozen, became a little older, but only a little older. She was nearly twenty-one the day a prince, disguised as a minstrel, came singing to the

town that lay below the castle. He called himself
Xingu, which was not his name, and dangerous,
since the name began with X — and still does.
He was, quite properly, a thing of shreds and
patches, a ragged minstrel, singing for pennies and
the love of singing. Xingu, as he so rashly called
himself, was the youngest son of a powerful king,
but he had grown weary of rich attire and ban-
quets and tournaments and the available princesses
of his own realm, and yearned to find in a far land

the maiden of his dreams, singing as he went, learning the life of the lowly, and possibly slaying a dragon here and there.

At the sign of the Silver Swan, in the town below the castle, where taverners, travelers, tale-tellers, tosspots, troublemakers, and other towns-people were gathered, he heard of Saralinda, loveliest princess on all the thousand islands of the ocean seas. "If you can turn the rain to silver, she is yours," a taverner leered.

"If you can slay the thorny Boar of Borythorn, she is yours," grinned a traveler. "But there is no thorny Boar of Borythorn, which makes it hard."

"What makes it even harder is her uncle's scorn and sword," sneered a tale-teller. "He will slit you from your guggle to your zatch."

"The Duke is seven feet, nine inches tall, and only twenty-eight years old, or in his prime," a tosspot gurgled. "His hand is cold enough to stop a clock, and strong enough to choke a bull, and swift enough to catch the wind. He breaks up minstrels in his soup, like crackers."

"Our minstrel here will warm the old man's heart with song, dazzle him with jewels and gold," a troublemaker simpered. "He'll trample on the Duke's camellias, spill his wine, and blunt his sword, and say his name begins with X, and in the end the Duke will say, 'Take Saralinda, with my blessing, O lordly Prince of Rags and Tags, O rider of the sun!'"

The troublemaker weighed eighteen stone, but the minstrel picked him up and tossed him in the air and caught him and set him down again. Then he paid his due and left the Swan.

"I've seen that youth before," the traveler mused, staring after Xingu, "but he was neither ragamuffin then, nor minstrel. Now let me see, where was it?"

"In his soup," the tosspot said, "like crackers."

II

UTSIDE the tavern the night was lighted by a rocking yellow moon that held a white star in its horn. In the gloomy castle on the hill a lantern gleamed and darkened, came and went, as if the gaunt Duke stalked from room to room, stabbing bats and spiders, killing mice. "Dazzle the Duke with jewels," the minstrel said aloud. "There's something in it somewhere, but what it is and where, I cannot think." He wondered if the Duke would order him to cause a fall of purple snow, or make a table out of sawdust, or merely slit him from his guggle to his zatch, and say to Saralinda,

"There he lies, your latest fool, a nameless minstrel. I'll have my varlets feed him to the geese."
The minstrel shuddered in the moonlight, wondering where his zatch and guggle were. He
wondered how and why and when he could
invade the castle. A duke was never known to
ask a ragged minstrel to his table, or set a task
for him to do, or let him meet a princess. "I'll
think of some way," thought the Prince. "I'll
think of something."

The hour was late, and revelers began to reel
and stagger home from inns and taverns, none in
rags, and none in tags, and some in velvet gowns.
One third of the dogs in town began to bark.
The minstrel took his lute from his shoulder and

improvised a song. He had thought of something.

"Hark, hark, the dogs do bark,
But only one in three.
They bark at those in velvet gowns,
They never bark at me."

A tale-teller, tottering home to bed, laughed at the song, and troublemakers and tosspots began to gather and listen.

"The Duke is fond of velvet gowns,
He'll ask you all to tea.
But I'm in rags, and I'm in tags,
He'll never send for me."

The townspeople crowded around the minstrel, laughing and cheering. "He's a bold one, Rags is, makin' songs about the Duke!" giggled a strutfurrow who had joined the crowd. The minstrel went on singing.

"Hark, hark, the dogs do bark,
The Duke is fond of kittens.
He likes to take their insides out,
And use their fur for mittens."

The crowd fell silent in awe and wonder, for

28

the townspeople knew the Duke had slain eleven men for merely staring at his hands, hands that were gloved in velvet gloves, bright with rubies and with diamonds. Fearing to be seen in the doomed and desperate company of the mad minstrel, the revelers slunk off to their homes to tell their wives. Only the traveler, who thought he had seen the singer some otherwhere and time, lingered to warn him of his peril. "I've seen you shining in the lists," he said, "or toppling knights in battle, or breaking men in two like crackers.

You must be Tristram's son, or Lancelot's, or are you Tyne or Tora?"

"A wandering minstrel, I," the minstrel said, "a thing of shreds and zatches." He bit his tongue in consternation at the slip it made.

"Even if you were the mighty Zorn of Zorna," said the man, "you could not escape the fury of the Duke. He'll slit you from your guggle to your zatch, from here to here." He touched the minstrel's stomach and his throat.

"I now know what to guard," the minstrel sighed.

A black figure in velvet mask and hood and

cloak disappeared behind a tree. "The cold Duke's spy-in-chief," the traveler said, "a man named Whisper. Tomorrow he will die." The minstrel waited. "He'll die because, to name your sins, he'll have to mention mittens. I leave at once for other lands, since I have mentioned mittens." He sighed. "You'll never live to wed his niece. You'll only die to feed his geese. Goodbye, good night, and sorry."

The traveler vanished, like a fly in the mouth of a frog, and the minstrel was left alone in the dark, deserted street. Somewhere a clock dropped a stony chime into the night. The minstrel began to sing again. A soft finger touched his shoulder and he turned to see a little man smiling in the moonlight. He wore an indescribable hat, his eyes were wide and astonished, as if everything were happening for the first time, and he had a dark, describable beard. "If you have nothing better than your songs," he said, "you are somewhat less than much, and only a little more than anything."

"I manage in my fashion," the minstrel said, and he strummed his lute and sang.

"Hark, hark, the dogs do bark,

The cravens are going to bed.

Some will rise and greet the sun,

But Whisper will be dead."

The old man lost his smile.

"Who are you?" the minstrel asked.

"I am the Golux," said the Golux, proudly, "the only Golux in the world, and not a mere Device."

"You resemble one," the minstrel said, "as Saralinda resembles the rose."

"I resemble only half the things I say I don't," the Golux said. "The other half resemble me." He sighed. "I must always be on hand when people are in peril."

"My peril is my own," the minstrel said.

"Half of it is yours and half is Saralinda's."

"I hadn't thought of that," the minstrel said. "I place my faith in you, and where you lead, I follow."

"Not so fast," the Golux said. "Half the places I have been to, never were. I make things up. Half the things I say are there cannot be found. When I was young I told a tale of buried gold, and men from leagues around dug in the woods. I dug myself."

"But why?"

"I thought the tale of treasure might be true."

"You said you made it up."

"I know I did, but then I didn't know I had. I forget things, too." The minstrel felt a vague uncertainty. "I make mistakes, but I am on the side of Good," the Golux said, "by accident and happenchance. I had high hopes of being Evil when I was two, but in my youth I came upon a firefly burning in a spider's web. I saved the victim's life."

"The firefly's?" said the minstrel.

"The spider's. The blinking arsonist had set the web on fire." The minstrel's uncertainty increased, but as he thought to slip away, a deep bell sounded in the castle and many lights appeared, and voices shouted orders and commands. A stream of lanterns started flowing down the darkness. "The Duke has heard your songs," the Golux said. "The fat is in the fire, the die is cast, the jig is up, the goose is cooked, and the cat is out of the bag."

"My hour has struck," the minstrel said. They heard a faint and distant rasping sound, as if a blade of steel were being sharpened on a stone.

"The Duke prepares to feed you to his geese," the Golux said. "We must invent a tale to stay his hand."

"What manner of tale?" the minstrel asked.

"A tale," the Golux said, "to make the Duke believe that slaying you would light a light in someone else's heart. He hates a light in people's hearts. So you must say a certain prince and princess can't be wed until the evening of the second day after the Duke has fed you to his geese."

"I wish that you would not keep saying that," the minstrel said.

"The tale sounds true," the Golux said, "and

very like a witch's spell. The Duke has awe of witches' spells. I'm certain he will stay his hand, I think."

The sound of tramping feet came near and nearer. The iron guards of the Duke closed in, their lanterns gleaming and their spears and armor. "Halt!" There was a clang and clanking.

"Do not arrest my friend," the youth implored.

"What friend?" the captain growled.

The minstrel looked around him and about, but there was no one there. A guard guffawed

and said, "Maybe he's seen the Golux."

"There isn't any Golux. I have been to school, and know," the captain said. The minstrel's uncertainty increased again. "Fall in!" the captain bawled. "Dress up that line."

"You heard him. Dress it up," the sergeant said. They marched the minstrel to the dungeon in the castle. A stream of lantern light flowed slowly up the hill.

III

T WAS morning. The cold Duke gazed out a window of the castle, as if he were watching flowers in bloom or flying birds. He was watching his varlets feeding Whisper to the geese. He turned away and took three limps and stared at the minstrel, standing in the great hall of the castle, both hands bound behind him. "What manner of prince is this you speak of, and what manner of maiden does he love, to use a word that makes no sense and has no point?" His voice sounded like iron dropped on velvet.

"A noble prince, a noble lady," the minstrel

said. "When they are wed a million people will be glad."

The Duke took his sword out of his sword-cane and stared at it. He limped across and faced his captive, and touched his guggle softly with the point, and touched his zatch, and sighed and frowned, and put the sword away. "We shall think of some amusing task for you to do," he said. "I do not like your tricks and guile. I think there is no prince or maiden who would wed if I should slay you, but I am neither sure nor certain." He grinned and said again, "We'll think of some amusing task for you to do."

"But I am not a prince," the minstrel said, "and only princes may aspire to Saralinda's hand."

The cold Duke kept on grinning. "Why, then we'll make a prince of you," he said. "The prince of Rags and Jingles." He clapped his gloves together and two varlets appeared without a word or sound. "Take him to his dungeon," said the Duke. "Feed him water without bread, and bread without water."

The varlets were taking the minstrel out of the great hall when down the marble stairs the Princess Saralinda floated like a cloud. The Duke's eye gleamed like crystal. The minstrel gazed in wonder. The Princess Saralinda was tall, with freesias in her dark hair, and she wore serenity brightly like the rainbow. It was not easy to tell her mouth from the rose, or her brow from the white lilac. Her voice was faraway music, and her eyes were candles burning on a tranquil night. She moved across the room like wind in violets, and her laughter sparkled on the air, which, from her presence, gained a faint and undreamed fragrance. The Prince was frozen by her beauty, but not cold, and the Duke, who was cold but not frozen, held up the palms of his gloves, as if she were a fire at which to warm his hands. The minstrel saw the blood come warmly to the lame man's cheeks. "This thing of rags and tags and tatters will play our little game," he told his niece, his voice like iron on velvet.

"I wish him well," the Princess said.

The minstrel broke his bonds and took her hand in his, but it was slashed away by the swift cane of the Duke. "Take him to his dungeon now," he said. He stared coldly at the minstrel through his monocle. "You'll find the most amusing bats and spiders there."

"I wish him well," the Princess said again, and the varlets took the minstrel to his dungeon.

When the great iron door of the dungeon clanked behind the minstrel, he found himself alone in blackness. A spider, swinging on a strand of web, swung back and forth. The zickering of bats was echoed by the walls. The minstrel took a step, avoiding snakes, and something squirmed. "Take care," the Golux said, "you're on my foot."

"Why are you here?" the minstrel cried.

"I forgot something. I forgot about the task the Duke will set you."

The minstrel thought of swimming lakes too wide to swim, of turning liquids into stone, or finding boneless creatures made of bone. "How came you here?" he asked. "And can you leave?"

"I never know," the Golux said. "My mother was a witch, but rather mediocre in her way. When she tried to turn a thing to gold, it turned to clay; and when she changed her rivals into fish, all she ever got was mermaids." The minstrel's heart was insecure. "My father was a wiz-

ard," said his friend, "who often cast his spells upon himself, when he was in his cups. Strike a light or light a lantern! Something I have hold of has no head."

The minstrel shuddered. "The task," he said. "You came to tell me."

"I did? Oh, yes. My father lacked the power of concentration, and that is bad for monks and priests, and worse for wizards. Listen. Tell the Duke that you will hunt the Boar, or travel thrice around the moon, or turn November into June. Implore him not to send you out to find a thousand jewels."

"And then?"

"And then he'll send you out to find a thousand jewels."

"But I am poor!" the minstrel cried.

"Come, come," the Golux said. "You're Zorn of Zorna. I had it from a traveler I met. It came to him as he was leaving town. Your father's casks and coffers shine with rubies and with sapphires."

"My father lives in Zorna," said the Prince, "and it would take me nine and ninety days: three and thirty days to go, and three and thirty days to come back here."

"That's six and sixty."

"It always takes my father three and thirty days to make decisions," said the Prince. "In spells and labors a certain time is always set, and I might be at sea when mine expires."

"That's another problem for another day," the Golux said. "Time is for dragonflies and angels. The former live too little and the latter live too long."

Zorn of Zorna thought awhile and said, "The task seems strange and simple."

"There are no jewels," the Golux said, "within the reach and ranges of this island, except the gems here in this castle. The Duke knows not that you are Zorn of Zorna. He thinks you are a minstrel without a penny or a moonstone. He's fond of jewels. You've seen them on his gloves."

The Prince stepped on a turtle. "The Duke has

spies," he said, "who may know who I am."

The Golux sighed. "I may be wrong," he said, "but we must risk and try it."

The Prince sighed in his turn. "I wish you could be surer."

"I wish I could," the Golux said. "My mother was born, I regret to say, only partly in a caul. I've saved a score of princes in my time. I cannot save them all." Something that would have been purple, if there had been light to see it by, scuttled across the floor. "The Duke might give me only thirty days, or forty-two, to find a thousand

jewels," said Zorn of Zorna. "Why should he give me ninety-nine?"

"The way I figure it," the Golux said, "is this. The longer the labor lasts, the longer lasts his gloating. He loves to gloat, you know."

The Prince sat down beside a toad. "My father may have lost his jewels," he said, "or given them away."

"I thought of that," the Golux said. "But I have other plans than one. Right now we have to sleep."

They found a corner without creatures and slept until the town clock struck the midnight hour.

Chains clanked and rattled, and the great iron door began to move. "The Duke has sent for you again," the Golux said. "Be careful what you say and what you do."

The great iron door began to open slowly. "When shall I see you next?" Zorn whispered. There was no answer. The Prince groped around

in the dark and felt a thing very like a cat, and touched the thing without a head, but he could not find the Golux.

The great iron door was open wide now and the dungeon filled with lantern light.

"The Duke commands your presence," growled a guard. "What was *that?*"

"What was what?"

"I know not," said the guard. "I thought I heard the sound of someone laughing."

"Is the Duke afraid of laughter?" asked the Prince.

"The Duke is not afraid of anything. Not even," said the guard, "the Todal."

"The Todal?"

"The Todal."

"What's the Todal?"

A lock of the guard's hair turned white and his teeth began to chatter. "The Todal looks like a blob of glup," he said. "It makes a sound like rabbits screaming, and smells of old, unopened rooms. It's waiting for the Duke to fail in some

50

endeavor, such as setting you a task that you can do."

"And if he sets me one, and I succeed?" the Prince inquired.

"The Blob will glup him," said the guard. "It's an agent of the devil, sent to punish evil-doers for having done less evil than they should. I talk too much. Come on. The Duke is waiting."

IV

HE DUKE sat at one end of a black oak table in the black oak room, lighted by flaming torches that threw red gleams on shields and lances. The Duke's gloves sparkled when he moved his hands. He stared moodily through his monocle at young Prince Zorn. The Duke sneered, which made him even colder. "So you would hunt the Boar," he said, "or travel thrice around the moon, or turn November into June." He laughed, and a torch went out. "Saralinda in November turns November into June. A cow can travel thrice around the moon, or even more. And *anyone* can merely *hunt* the Boar. I have another plan for you. I thought it up myself last night, while I was killing mice. I'll send you out to find a thousand jewels and bring them back."

The Prince turned pale, or tried to. "A wandering minstrel, I," he said, "a thing of—"

"Rubies and sapphires." The Duke's chuckle sounded like ice cackling in a cauldron. "For you are Zorn of Zorna," he whispered, softly. "Your father's casks and vaults and coffers shine with jewels. In six and sixty days you could sail to Zorna and return."

"It always takes my father three and thirty days to make decisions," cried the Prince.

The Duke grinned. "That is what I wanted to know, my naïve Prince," he said. "Then you would have me give you nine and ninety days?"

"That would be fair," the Prince replied. "But how do you know that I am Zorn?"

"I have a spy named Hark," the Duke explained, "who found your princely raiment in your quarters in the town and brought it here,

53

with certain signs and seals and signatures, revealing who you are. Go put the raiment on." He pointed at a flight of iron stairs. "You'll find it in a chamber on whose door a star is turning black. Don it and return. I'll think of beetles while you're gone, and things like that." The Duke limped to his chair and sat down again, and the Prince started up the iron stairs, wondering where the Golux was. He stopped and turned and said, "You will not give me nine and ninety days. How many, then?" The Duke sneered. "I'll think of a lovely number," he said. "Go on."

When Zorn came back he wore his royal attire, but the Duke's spies had sealed his sword, so that he could not draw it. The Duke sat staring at a man who wore a velvet mask and cloak and hood. "This is Hark," he said, "and this is Listen." He gestured with his cane at nothing.

"There's no one there," said Zorn.

"Listen is invisible," the Duke explained. "Listen can be heard, but never seen. They are here to learn the mark and measure of your task. I give you nine and ninety hours, not nine and ninety days, to find a thousand jewels and bring them here. When you return, the clocks must all be striking five."

"The clocks here in the castle?" asked the Prince. "The thirteen clocks?"

"The clocks here in the castle," said the Duke, "the thirteen clocks."

The Prince looked at the two clocks on the walls. Their hands pointed to ten minutes of five. "The hands are frozen," said the Prince. "The clocks are dead."

"Precisely," said the Duke, "and what is more, which makes your task a charming one, there are no jewels that could be found within the space of nine and ninety hours, except those in my vaults, and these." He held his gloves up and they sparkled.

"A pretty task," said Hark.

"Ingenious," said the voice of Listen.

"I thought you'd like it," said the Duke. "Unseal his sword." Invisible hands unsealed the Prince's sword.

"And if I should succeed?" asked Zorn.

The Duke waved a gloved hand at the iron stairs, and Zorn saw Saralinda standing there. "I wish him well," she said, and her uncle laughed and looked at Zorn. "I hired a witch," he said, "to cast a tiny spell upon her. When she is in my presence, all that she can say is this: 'I wish him well.' You like it?"

"A clever spell," said Hark.

"An awful spell," the voice of Listen said.

The Prince and Princess spoke a silent language

with their eyes, until the Duke cried, "Go!" and Saralinda vanished up the stairs.

"And if I fail?" asked Zorn.

The Duke removed his sword from his sword-cane and ran his glove along the blade. "I'll slit you from your guggle to your zatch, and feed you to the Todal."

"I've heard of it," said Zorn.

The Duke smiled. "You've only heard of half

of it," he said. "The other half is worse. It's made
of lip. It feels as if it had been dead at least a dozen
days, but it moves about like monkeys and like
shadows." The Prince took out his sword and put
it back. "The Todal can't be killed," the Duke said,
softly.

"It gleeps," said Hark.

"What's gleeping?" asked the Prince.

The Duke and Hark and Listen laughed. "Time

59

is wasting, Prince," the Duke reminded him. "Already you have only eight and ninety hours. I wish you every strangest kind of luck." A wide oak door suddenly opened at the end of the room, and the Prince saw lightning and midnight and falling rain. "One last word and warning," said the Duke. "I would not trust the Golux overfar. He cannot tell what can be from what can't. He seldom knows what should be from what is."

The Prince glanced at Hark and at the Duke, and at a spot where he thought Listen stood. "When all the clocks are striking five," he said, and left the room. The laughter of the Duke and Hark and Listen followed him out the door and down the stairs and into the darkness. When he had gone a few steps from the castle, he looked up at a lighted window and thought he saw the Princess Saralinda standing there. A rose fell at his feet, and as he picked it up, the laughter of the Duke and Hark and Listen increased inside the black oak room and died away.

V

HE PRINCE had gone but a short way from the castle when he felt a gentle finger touch his elbow. "It is the Golux," said the Golux, proudly. "The only Golux in the world."

The Prince was in no mood for the old man's gaiety and cheer. The Golux did not seem wonderful to him now, and even his indescribable hat was suddenly describable. "The Duke thinks you are not so wise as he thinks you think you are," he said.

The Golux smiled. "I think he is not so wise as he thinks I think he is," he said. "I was there. I know the terms. I had thought that only dragon-

flies and angels think of time, never having been
an angel or a dragonfly."

"How were you there?" the Prince said in surprise.

"I am Listen," the Golux said, "or at any rate,
he thinks I am. Never trust a spy you cannot see.
The Duke is lamer than I am old, and I am shorter
than he is cold, but it comes to you with some surprise that I am wiser than he is wise."

The Prince's courage began to return. "I think

63

you are the most remarkable man in the world," he said.

"Who thought not so a moment since, knows not the apple from the quince," the Golux said He scowled. "We now have only eight and ninety *hours* to find a thousand gems," he said.

"You said that you had other plans than one," the Prince reminded him.

"What plans?" the Golux asked.

"You didn't say," said Zorn.

The Golux closed his eyes and clasped his hands. "There was a treasure ship that sank, not more than forty hours from here," he said. "But, come to think of it, the Duke ransacked the ship and stole the jewels."

"So much," sighed Zorn, "for that."

The Golux thought again. "If there were hail," he said, "and we could stain the hail with blood, it might turn into rubies."

"There is no hail," said Zorn.

The Golux sighed. "So much," he said, "for that."

"The task is hard," said Zorn, "and can't be done."

"I can do a score of things that can't be done," the Golux said. "I can find a thing I cannot see and see a thing I cannot find. The first is time, the second is a spot before my eyes. I can feel a thing I cannot touch and touch a thing I cannot feel. The first is sad and sorry, the second is your heart. What would you do without me? Say 'nothing.'"

"Nothing," said the Prince.

"Good. Then you're helpless and I'll help you. I said I had another plan than one, and I have just remembered what it is. There is a woman on this isle, who'd have some eight and eighty years, and she is gifted with the strangest gift of all. For when she weeps, what do you think she weeps?"

"Tears," said Zorn.

"Jewels," said the Golux.

The Prince stared at him. "But that is too remarkable to be," he said.

"I don't see why," the Golux said. "Even the

65

lowly oyster makes his pearls without the use of eyes or hands or any tools, and pearls are jewels. The oyster is a blob of glup, but a woman is a woman."

The Prince thought of the Todal and felt a small cold feeling in his guggle. "Where does this wondrous woman dwell?" he asked.

The old man groaned. "Over mountain, over stream, by the way of storm and thunder, in a hut so high or deep—I never can remember which—the naked eye can't see it." He stood up. "We must be on our way," he said. "It will take us ninety hours, or more or less, to go and come. It's this way, or it's that way. Make up my mind."

"How can I?" asked the Prince. "You have a rose," the Golux said. "Hold it in your hand." The Prince took out the rose and held it in his hand, and its stem slowly turned and stopped. "It's this way," cried the Golux, and they started off in the direction the stem of the rose had pointed out. "I will tell you the tale of Hagga," said the Golux.

When Hagga was eleven (he began) and picking cherries in the woods one day, and asphodel, she came upon the good King Gwain of Yarrow with his foot caught in a wolf trap. "Weep for me, maiden," said the King, "for I am ludicrous and laughable, with my foot caught in this trap. I am no longer ert, for I have lost my ertia. By twiddling my fingers or clapping my hands, I have often changed the fate of men, but now I cannot get my foot loose from this thing."

"I have no time for tears," the maiden said. She knew the secret of the trap, and was about to free the fettered foot, when a farmer from a near-by farm began to laugh. The King beshrewed him

and his wife, and turned them into grasshoppers, creatures that look as if their feet were caught in traps, even when they aren't.

"Lo, the maid has freed my foot," the King exulted, seeing that she had, "but it is numb, and feels like someone else's foot, not mine." The maiden took off his shoe and rubbed his foot, until it felt like his and he could put it down. And for her kindness the grateful King gave her the power to weep jewels when she wept, instead of tears. When the people learned of the strange gift the King had given Hagga, they came from leagues around, by night and day, in warm and winter weather, to make her sad and sorry. Nothing tragic happened but she heard of it and wept. People came with heavy hearts and left with pearls and rubies. Paths were paved with pearls, and rivers ran with rubies. Children played with sapphires

in the streets, and dogs chewed opals. Every pea-
cock had at least nine diamonds in its gizzard, and
one, cut open on St. Wistow's Day, had thirty-
eight. The price of stones and pebbles rose, the
price of gems declined, until, by making Hagga
weep, you could be hanged and fined. In the end,
the jewels were melted, in a frightful fire, by order
of the King. "I will make her weep myself, one
day each year," the King decreed, "and thus and
hence, the flow of gems will make some sense,
and have some point and balance." But alas, and
but alack, the maid could weep no more at any
tale of tragedy or tribulation. Damsels killed by
dragons left her cold, and broken hearts, and child-

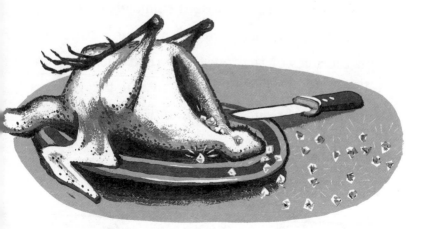

ren lost, and love denied. She never wept by day or night, in warm or winter weather. She grew to be sixteen, and twenty-six, and thirty-four, and forty-eight, and fifty-two, and now she waits, at eighty-eight, for me and you. "I hope," the Golux said, "that this is true. I make things up, you know."

The young Prince sighed and said, "I know you do. If Hagga weeps no more, why should she weep for you?"

The Golux thought it over. "I feel that she is frail and fragile. I trust that she is sad and sorry. I hope that she is neither dead nor dying. I'll think of something very sad to tell her. Very sad and lonely. Take out your rose, I think we're lost."

They had become tangled in brambles by now, and the trees of the forest they had entered were tall and thick. Thorns began to tear the Prince's raiment. Lightning flashed and thunder rolled, and all paths vanished. The Prince took out the rose and held it in his hand. The stem began to turn and twist, and pointed.

"Around this way," the Golux said. "It's lighter here." He found a narrow path that led straight onward. As they walked along the path, the Golux leading, they met a Jackadandy, whose clothes were torn and tattered.

"I told my tales to Hagga," said the man; "but Hagga weeps no more. I told her tales of lovers lost in April. I told her tales of maidens dead in June. I told her tales of princes fed to geese. I even told her how I lost my youngest niece."

"This is sad," the Golux said, "and getting sadder."

"The way is long," the torn man said, "and getting longer. The road goes uphill all the way, and even farther. I wish you luck," he said. "You'll need it." He disappeared in brambles.

The only light in the forest came from lightning, and when it flashed they watched the rose and followed where it pointed. This brought them, on the second day, into a valley. They saw a Jack-o'-lent approaching, his clothes all torn and tattered. "I told my tales to Hagga," said the man, "but Hagga weeps no more. I told her tales of lovers lost at sea and drowned in fountains. I told her tales of babies lost in woods and lost on mountains. She wept not," said the Jack-o'-lent. "The way is dark, and getting darker. The hut is high and even higher. I wish you luck. There is none." He vanished in the briars.

The brambles and the thorns grew thick and thicker in a ticking thicket of bickering crickets. Farther along and stronger, bonged the gongs of a throng of frogs, green and vivid on their lily pads. From the sky came the crying of flies, and the pilgrims leaped over a bleating sheep creeping knee-deep in a sleepy stream, in which swift and slippery snakes slid and slithered silkily, whispering sinful secrets.

A comet whistled through the sky, and by its light they saw the hut of Hagga high on Hagga's hill. "If she is dead, there may be strangers there," the Golux said.

"How many hours do we have left?" the Prince demanded.

"If we can make her weep within the hour," the Golux said, "we'll barely make it."

"I hope that she's alive and sad," said Zorn.

"I feel that she has died," the Golux sighed. "I feel it in my stomach. You better carry me. I'm weary."

Zorn of Zorna picked the Golux up and carried him.

VI

T WAS cold on Hagga's hill, and fresh with furrows where the dragging points of stars had plowed the fields. A peasant in a purple smock stalked the smoking furrows, sowing seeds. There was a smell, the Golux thought, a little like Forever in the air, but mixed with something faint and less enduring, possibly the fragrance of a flower. "There's no light in her window," the Golux said, "and it is dark and getting darker."

"There's no smoke in her chimney," said the Prince, "and it is cold and getting colder."

The Golux barely breathed and said, "What worries me the most is that spider's web there on

76

the door, that stretches from the hinges to the latch."

The young Prince felt a hollow feeling in his zatch. "Knock on her door," the Golux said, his voice so high it quavered. He crossed his fingers and kept them crossed, and Zorn knocked on the door. No one answered. "Knock again," the Golux cried, and Prince Zorn knocked again.

Hagga was there. She came to the door and stared at them, a woman neither dead nor dying, and clearly only thirty-eight or thirty-nine. The Golux had missed her age by fifty years, as old men often do. "Weep for us," the Golux cried, "or else this Prince will never wed his Princess."

"I have no tears," said Hagga. "Once I wept when ships were overdue, or brooks ran dry, or tangerines were overripe, or sheep got something in their eye. I weep no more," said Hagga. Her eyes were dry as deserts and her mouth seemed made of stone. "I have turned a thousand persons gemless from my door. Come in," she said. "I weep no more."

The room was dark and held a table and a chair, and in one corner something like a chest, made of oak and bound with brass. The Golux smiled and then looked sad, and said, "I have tales to make a hangman weep, and tales to bring a tear of sorrow to a monster's eye. I have tales that would disturb a dragon's sleep, and even make the Todal sigh."

At the mention of the Todal, Hagga's hair turned gray. "Once I wept when maids were married underneath the April moon. I weep no more when maids are buried, even in the month of June."

"You have the emotions of a fish," said the Golux, irritably. He sat on the floor and told her tales of the death of kings, and kindred things, and little children choked by rings.

"I have no tears," said Hagga.

He told her tales of the frogs in the forum, and the toads in the rice that destroyed the poppycockalorum and the cockahoopatrice.

"I weep no more," said Hagga.

"Look," the Golux said, "and listen! The Princess Saralinda will never wed this youth until the

day he lays a thousand jewels upon a certain table."

"I would weep for Saralinda," Hagga sighed, "if I were able."

The Prince had wandered to the oaken chest. He seized its cover with his hand and threw it open. A radiance filled the room and lit the darkest corners. Inside the chest there were at least ten thousand jewels of the very sort and kind the Duke demanded. Diamonds flared and rubies glowed, and sapphires burned and emeralds seemed on fire. They looked at Hagga. "These are the jewels of laughter," Hagga said. "I woke up fourteen days ago to find them on my bed. I had laughed until I wept at something in my sleep." The Golux grabbed a gleaming handful of the gems, and then another, crowing with delight. "Put them back," said Hagga. "For there's a thing that you must know, concerning jewels of laughter. They always turn again to tears a fortnight after. It has been a fortnight, to the day and minute, since I took the pretties to this chest and put them in it."

Even as they watched, the light and color died. The diamonds dimmed, the emeralds went out, and the jewels of Hagga's laughter turned to tears, with a little sound like sighing. There was nothing in the chest but limpid liquid, leering up at them and winking. "You must think," the Golux cried. "You must think of what you laughed at in your sleep."

Hagga's eyes were blank. "I do not know, for this was fourteen days ago."

"Think!" the Golux said.

"Think!" said Zorn of Zorna.

Hagga frowned and said, "I never can remember dreams."

The Golux clasped his hands behind his back and thought it over. "As I remember and recall," he said, "the jewels of sorrow last forever. Such was the gift and power the good Gwain gave you. What was he doing, by the way, so many leagues from Yarrow?"

"Hunting," Hagga said. "Wolves, as I recall it."

The Golux scowled. "I am a man of logic, in my way. What happened on that awful day, to make him value sorrow over and above the gift of laughter? Why have these jewels turned to tears a fortnight after?"

"There was a farmer from a near-by farm, who laughed," said Hagga. "'On second thought,' the good King said, 'I will amend and modify the gift I gave you. The jewels of sorrow will last beyond all measure, but may the jewels of laughter give you little pleasure.'"

The Golux groaned. "If there's one thing in the world I hate," he said, "it is amendments." His eyes turned bright and brighter, and he clapped his hands. "I will make her laugh until she weeps," he said.

The Golux told her funny tales of things that were and had been, but Hagga's eyes were dry as quartz and her mouth seemed made of agate. "I laugh at nothing that has been," she said, "or is."

The Golux smiled. "Then we will think of things that will be, and aren't now, and never

were. I'll think of something," and he thought,
and thought of something.

> "A dehoy who was terribly hobble,
> Cast only stones that were cobble
> And bats that were ding,
> From a shot that was sling,
> But never hit inks that were bobble."

Hagga laughed until she wept, and seven moon-
stones trickled down her cheek and clattered on

the floor. "She's weeping semiprecious stones!" the
Golux wailed. He tried again:

> "There was an old coddle so molly,
> He talked in a glot that was poly,
> His gaws were so gew
> That his laps became dew,
> And he ate only pops that were lolly."

Hagga laughed until she wept, and seven brilliants
trickled down her cheek and clattered on the floor.
"Rhinestones!" groaned the Golux. "Now she's
weeping costume jewelry!"

The young Prince tried his hand at telling tales
of laughter, but for his pains he got a shower of
tourmaline, a cat's-eye, and a flux of pearls. "The
Duke hates pearls," the Golux moaned. "He thinks
they're made by fish."

It grew darker in the room and they could
scarcely see. The starlight and the moon were gone.
They stood there, still as statues. The Golux
cleared his throat. The Prince uncrossed his arms
and crossed them. And then, without a rhyme or
reason, out of time and out of season, Hagga

laughed and kept on laughing. No one had said a
word, no one had told a tale. It might have been
the hooting of an owl. It might have been the
crawling of a snail. But Hagga laughed and kept
on laughing, and precious jewels twinkled down
her cheek and sparkled on the floor, until the hut
was ankle-deep in diamonds and in rubies. The
Golux counted out a thousand and put them in
a velvet sack that he had brought along. "I wish
that she had laughed," he sighed, "at something I
had said."

Zorn of Zorna took her hand. "God keep you warm in winter," said the Prince, "and cool in summer."

"Farewell," the Golux said, "and thank you."

Hagga laughed and kept on laughing, and sapphires burned upon the floor and lit the Golux toward the door.

"How many hours are left us now?" the young Prince cried "It's odd," the Golux muttered to himself. "I could have sworn that she had died. This is the only time my stomach ever lied."

"How many hours are left us now?" the Prince implored.

Hagga sat upon the chest and kept on laughing.

"I should say," the Golux said, "that we have only forty left, but it is downhill all the way.

They went out into the moonless night and peered about them in the dark.

"I think it's this way," the Golux said, and they went the way he thought it was.

"What about the clocks?" demanded Zorn.

The Golux exhaled a sorry breath. "That's another problem for another hour," he said.

Inside the hut, something red and larger than a ruby glowed among the jewels and Hagga picked it up. "A rose," she said. "They must have dropped it."

VII

N THE black oak room the yellow torches flared and crackled on the walls, and their fire burned on the lances and the shields. The Duke's gloves glittered. "How goes the night?" he gnarled.

"The moon is down," said Hark. "I have not heard the clocks."

"You'll never hear them!" screamed the Duke. "I slew time in this castle many a cold and snowy year ago."

Hark stared at him emptily and seemed to be chewing something. "Time froze here. Someone left the windows open."

"Bah!" The Duke sat down at the far end of

the table, stood up again, and limped about. "It
bled hours and minutes on the floor. I saw it with
my eye." Hark kept on chewing something. Outside the Gothic windows thunder growled. An
owl flew by.

"There are no jewels," roared the Duke.
"They'll have to bring me pebbles from the sea or
mica from the meadows." He gave his awful
laugh. "How goes the night?" he asked again.

"I have been counting off and on," said Hark, "and I should say they have some forty minutes left."

"They'll never make it!" the cold Duke screamed. "I hope they drowned, or broke their legs, or lost their way." He came so close to Hark their noses almost touched. "Where were they going?" he whispered harshly.

Hark stepped backward seven steps. "I met a Jackadandy, some seven hours ago," he said. "They passed him on their way to Hagga's hill. Do you remember Hagga, and have you thought of her?"

The Duke's loud laughter rang the shields.

"Hagga weeps no more," he said. "Hagga has no tears. She did not even weep when she was told about the children locked up in my tower."

"I hated that," said Hark.

"I liked it," said the Duke. "No child can sleep in my camellias." He began to limp again and stared out at the night. "Where is Listen?" he demanded.

"He followed them," said Hark, "the Golux and the Prince."

"I do not trust him," growled the Duke. "I like a spy that I can see. Let me have men about me that are visible." He shouted "Listen!" up the stairs, and "Listen!" out the windows, but no one answered. "I'm cold," he rasped.

"You always are."

"I'm colder," snarled the Duke, "and never tell me what I always am!" He took his sword out and slashed at nothing and at silence. "I miss Whisper."

"You fed him to the geese," said Hark. "They seemed to like him."

"Silence! What was that?"

"What did it sound like?"

"Like princes stealing up the stairs, like Saralinda leaving." The Duke limped to the iron stairs and slashed again at silence and at nothing. "What does he feel like? Have you felt him?"

"Listen? He's five feet high," said Hark. "He has a beard, and something on his head I can't describe."

"The Golux!" shrieked the Duke. "You felt the
Golux! I hired him as a spy and didn't know it."

A purple ball with gold stars on it came slowly bouncing down the iron stairs and winked and
twinkled, like a naked child saluting priests.
"What insolence is this?" the Duke demanded.
"What *is* that thing?"

"A ball," said Hark.

"I know that!" screamed the Duke. "But why?
What does its ghastly presence signify?"

"It looks to me," said Hark, "very like a ball the Golux and those children used to play with."

"They're on his side!" The Duke was apoplectic. "Their ghosts are on his side."

"He has a lot of friends," said Hark.

"Silence!" roared the Duke. "He knows not what is dead from what is dying, or where he's been from where he's going, or striking clocks from clocks that never strike."

"What makes me think he does?" The spy stopped chewing. Something very much like noth-

96

ing anyone had seen before came trotting down the stairs and crossed the room.

"What is that?" the Duke asked, palely.

"I don't know what it is," said Hark, "but it's the only one there ever was."

The Duke's gloved hands shook and shimmered. "I'll throw them up for grabs betwixt the Todal and the geese! I'll lock them in the dungeon with the thing without a head!" At the mention of the Todal, Hark's velvet mask turned gray. The Duke's eye twisted upward in its socket. "I'll slay

them all!" he said. "This sweetheart and her suitor, this cross-eyed clown! You hear me?"

"Yes," said Hark, "but there are rules and rites and rituals, older than the sound of bells and snow on mountains."

"Go on," the Duke said, softly, looking up the stairs.

"You must let them have their time and turn to make the castle clocks strike five."

"The castle clocks were murdered," said the Duke. "I killed time here myself one snowy morning. You still can see the old brown stains, where seconds bled to death, here on my sleeve." He laughed. "What else?" he asked.

"You know as well as I," said Hark. "The Prince must have his turn and time to lay a thousand jewels there on the table."

"And if he does?"

"He wins the hand of Princess Saralinda."

"The only warm hand in the castle," said the Duke. "Who loses Saralinda loses fire. I mean the fire of the setting suns, and not the cold and cheerless flame of jewels. Her eyes are candles burning in a shrine. Her feet appear to me as doves. Her fingers bloom upon her breast like flowers."

"This is scarcely the way," said Hark, "to speak of one's own niece."

"She's not my niece! I stole her!" cried the Duke. "I stole her from the castle of a king! I snatched her from the bosom of a sleeping queen. I still bear on my hands the marks of where she bit me."

"The Queen?" asked Hark.

"The Princess," roared the Duke.

"Who was the King?" asked Hark.

His master scowled. "I never knew," he said. "My ship was beached upon an island in a storm. There was no moon or any star. No lights were in the castle."

"How could you find the Princess then?" asked Hark.

"She had a radiance," said the Duke. "She shone there like a star upon her mother's breast. I knew I had to have that splendor in my castle. I

mean to keep her here till she is twenty-one. The day she is, I'll wed her, and that day is tomorrow."

"Why haven't you before?" asked Hark. "This castle is your kingdom."

The Duke smiled and showed his upper teeth.

"Because her nurse turned out to be a witch who cast a spell upon me."

"What were its terms?" asked Hark.

"I cannot wed her till the day she's twenty-one, and that day is tomorrow."

"You said that once before."

"I must keep her in a chamber where she is safe from me. I've done that."

"I like that part," said Hark.

"I hate it," snarled the Duke. "I must give and grant the right to any prince to seek her hand in marriage. I've done that, too." He sat down at the table.

"In spells of this sort," Hark said, chewing,

"one always finds a chink or loophole, by means of which the right and perfect prince can win her hand in spite of any task you set him. How did the witch announce that part of it?"

"Like this. 'She can be saved, and you destroyed, only by a prince whose name begins with X and doesn't.' There is no prince whose name begins with X and doesn't."

Hark's mask slipped off and he put it back again, but not before the Duke saw laughter in his eyes. "This prince," said Hark, "is Zorn of Zorna, but to your terror and distaste, he once posed as a minstrel. His name was Xingu then and wasn't. This is the prince whose name begins with X and doesn't."

The Duke's sword had begun to shake. "Nobody ever tells me anything," he whispered to himself.

Another ball came bouncing down the stairs, a black ball stamped with scarlet owls. The cold Duke watched it roll across the floor. "What impudence is this?" he cried.

Hark walked to the stairs and listened, and turned and said, "There's someone up there."

"It's the children!" croaked the Duke.

"The children are dead," said Hark, "and the sound I heard was made by living feet."

"How much time is left them?" cried the Duke.

"Half an hour, I think," said Hark.

"I'll have their guggles on my sword for playing games with me!" The Duke started up the stairs and stopped. "They're up there, all of them. Call out the guards," he barked.

"The guards are guarding the clocks," said Hark. "You wanted it that way. There are eleven guards, and each one guards a clock. You and I are guarding *these*." He pointed at the two clocks on the walls. "You wanted it that way."

"Call out the guards," the Duke repeated, and his agent called the guards. They trooped into the room like engines. The Duke limped up the stairs, his drawn sword shining. "Follow me!" he cried. "Another game's afoot! I'll slay the Golux and the Prince, and marry Saralinda!" He led the way. The guards ramped up the stairs like engines. Hark smiled, and chewed again, and followed.

The black oak room was silent for a space of seven seconds. Then a secret door swung open in a wall. The Golux slipped into the room. The Princess followed. His hands were raw and red from climbing vines to Saralinda's chamber. "How could you find the castle in the dark without my rose?" she asked. "He would not let me burn a torch."

"You lighted up your window like a star, and we could see the castle from afar," the Golux said. "Our time is marked in minutes. Start the clocks!"

"I cannot start the clocks," the Princess said.

They heard the sound of fighting far above. "He faces thirteen men," she cried, "and that is hard."

"We face thirteen clocks," the Golux said, "and that is harder. Start the clocks!"

"How can I start the clocks?" the Princess wailed.

"Your hand is warmer than the snow is cold," the Golux said. "Touch the first clock with your hand." The Princess touched it. Nothing happened. "Again!" Saralinda held her hand against the clock and nothing happened. "We are ruined," said the Golux simply, and Saralinda's heart stood still.

She cried, "Use magic!"

"I have no magic to depend on," groaned the Golux. "Try the other clock."

The Princess tried the other clock and nothing happened. "Use logic, then!" she cried. In the secret walls they heard the Iron Guard pounding after Zorn, and coming close.

"Now let me see," the Golux said. "If you can touch the clocks and never start them, then you can start the clocks and never touch them. That's logic, as I know and use it. Hold your hand this far away. Now that far. Closer! Now a little farther back. A little farther. There! I think you have it! Do not move!"

The clogged and rigid works of the clock began to whir. They heard a tick and then a ticking.

The Princess Saralinda fled from room to room, like wind in clover, and held her hand the proper distance from the clocks. Something like a vulture spread its wings and left the castle. "That was Then," the Golux said.

"It's Now!" cried Saralinda.

A morning glory that had never opened, opened in the courtyard. A cock that never crowed, began to crow. The light of morning stained the windows, and in the walls the cold

Duke moaned, "I hear the sound of time. And yet I slew it, and wiped my bloody sword upon its beard." He thought that Zorn of Zorna had escaped the guards. His sword kept whining in the blackness, and once he slashed his own left knee—he thought it was the Golux. "Come out, you crooning knave!" he cried. "Stand forward, Zorn of Zorna!"

"He's not here," said the spy.

They heard the savage clash of swords.

108

"They've got him!" squealed the Duke. "Eleven men to one!"

"You may have heard of Galahad," said Hark, "whose strength was as the strength of ten."

"That leaves one man to get him," cried the Duke. "I count on Krang, the strongest guard I have, the finest fencer in the world, save one. An unknown prince in armor vanquished him a year ago, somewhere on an island. No one else can do it."

"The unknown prince," said Hark, "was Zorn of Zorna."

"I'll slay him then myself!" The Duke's voice rose and echoed down the dark and secret stairs. "I slew time with the bloody hand that grips your arm, and time is greater far than Zorn of Zorna!"

Hark began to chew again. "No mortal man can murder time," he said, "and even if he could, there's something else: a clockwork in a maiden's heart, that strikes the hours of youth and love, and knows the southward swan from winter snow, and summer afternoons from tulip time."

"You sicken me with your chocolate chatter," snarled the Duke. "Your tongue is made of candy. I'll slay this ragged prince, if Krang has missed him. If there were light, I'd show you on my sleeves the old brown stains of seconds, where they bled and died. I slew time in these gloomy halls, and wiped my bloody blade—"

"Ah, shut up," said Hark. "You are the most aggressive villain in the world. I always meant to tell you that. I said it and I'm glad."

"Silence," roared the Duke. "Where are we?" They stumbled down the secret stairs.

"This is the hidden door," said Hark, "that leads into the oak room."

"Open," roared the Duke, his sword gripped in his hand. Hark groped and found the secret knob.

VIII

HE BLACK oak room was bright with flaming torches, but brighter with the light of Saralinda. The cold eye of the Duke was dazzled by the gleaming of a thousand jewels that sparkled on the table. His ears were filled with chiming as the clocks began to strike.

"One!" said Hark.

"Two!" cried Zorn of Zorna.

"Three!" the Duke's voice almost whispered.

"Four!" sighed Saralinda.

"Five!" the Golux crowed, and pointed at the table. "The task is done, the terms are met," he said.

The Duke's cold eye slowly moved around the

room. "Where are my guards?" he croaked, "and where is Krang, the greatest of them all?"

"I lured them to the tower," said Zorn, "and locked them in. The one that's tied in knots is Krang."

The Duke glared at the jewels on the table. "They're false!" he said. "They must be colored pebbles!" He picked one up, and saw that it was real, and put it down again.

"The task is done," said Hark, "the terms are met."

"Not until I count them," said the Duke. "If there be only one that isn't here, I wed the Princess Saralinda on the morrow." The figures in the room were still and he could hear their breathing.

"What a gruesome way to treat one's niece," the Golux cried.

"She's not my niece," the lame man sneered. "I stole her from a king." He showed his lower teeth. "We all have flaws," he said, "and mine is being wicked." He sat down at the table and began to count the gems.

"Who is my father then?" the Princess cried.

The spy's black eyebrows rose. "I thought the Golux told you, but then, of course, he never could remember things."

114

"Especially," the Golux said, "the names of kings."

"Your father," said the spy, "is good King Gwain of Yarrow."

"I knew that once," the Golux said, "but I forgot it." He turned to Saralinda. "Then the gift your father gave to Hagga has operated in the end to make you happy."

The Duke looked up and bared his teeth. "The tale is much too tidy for my taste," he snarled. "I hate it." He went on counting.

115

"It's neat," said Hark, "and, to *my* taste, refreshing." He removed his mask. His eyes were bright and jolly. "If I may introduce myself," he said, "I am a servant of the King, the good King Gwain of Yarrow."

"That," the Golux said, "I didn't know. You could have saved the Princess many years ago."

The servant of the King looked sad, and said, "This part I always hate to tell, but I was under a witch's spell."

"I weary of witches," the Golux said, "with due respect to Mother."

The Duke's smile showed his upper teeth. "I cannot even trust the spies I see," he muttered. His eye moved glassily around and saw the Golux. "You mere Device!" he gnarled. "You platitude! You Golux ex machina!"

"Quiet, please," the Golux said, "you gleaming thief."

"Nine hundred ninety-eight." The Duke was counting. "Nine hundred ninety-nine." He had counted all the jewels, and put them in a sack. There was none left on the table. He gave them all a look of horrid glee. "The Princess," said the Duke, "belongs to me."

A deathly silence filled the room. The Golux turned a little pale and his hand began to shake. He remembered something in the dark, coming down from Hagga's hill, that struck against his ankle, a sapphire or a ruby that had fallen from the the sack. "One thousand," groaned the Duke, in a tone of vast surprise. A diamond had fallen from his glove, the left one, and no one but the Golux saw it fall. The Duke stood up and sneered. "What are you waiting for?" he shrieked. "Depart! If you be gone forever, it will not be long enough! If you return no more, then it will be too soon!" He slowly turned to Zorn. "What kind of knots?" he snarled.

"Turk's head," the young Prince said. "I learned them from my sister."

"Begone!" the cold Duke screamed again, and bathed his hands in rubies. "My jewels," he croaked, "will last forever." The Golux, who had never tittered, tittered. The great doors of the oak room opened, and they left the cold Duke standing there, up to his wrists in diamonds.

"Yarrow," said the Prince, "is halfway on our journey." They stood outside the castle.

"You'll need these," said the Golux. He held the reins of two white horses. "Your ship lies in the harbor. It sails within the hour."

"It sails at midnight," Hark corrected him.

"I can't remember everything," the Golux said. "My father's clocks were always slow. He also lacked the power of concentration."

Zorn helped the Princess to her saddle. She gazed a last time at the castle. "A fair wind stands for Yarrow," said the Prince.

The Golux gazed a last time at the Princess. "Keep warm," he said. "Ride close together.

Remember laughter. You'll need it even in the blessed isles of Ever After."

"There are no horses in the stables," mused the Prince. "Whence came these white ones?"

"The Golux has a lot of friends," said Hark. "I guess they give him horses when he needs them. But on the other hand, he may have made them up. He makes things up, you know."

"I know he does," sighed Zorn of Zorna. "You sail for Yarrow with us?"

"I must stay a fortnight longer," Hark replied. "So runs my witch's spell. It will give me time to tidy up, and untie Krang as well."

They looked around for the old Device, but he was there no longer. "Where has he gone?" cried Saralinda.

"Oh," said Hark, "he knows a lot of places."

"Give him," Saralinda said, "my love, and this." Hark took the rose.

The two white horses snorted snowy mist in the cool green glade that led down to the harbor. A fair wind stood for Yarrow and, looking far to sea, the Princess Saralinda thought she saw, as people often think they see, on clear and windless days, the distant shining shores of Ever After. Your guess is quite as good as mine (there are a lot of things that shine) but I have always thought she did, and I will always think so.

EPILOGUE

FORTNIGHT later, the Duke was gloating over his jewels in the oak room when they suddenly turned to tears, with a little sound like sighing. The fringes of his glowing gloves were stained with Hagga's laughter. He staggered to his feet and drew his sword, and shouted, "Whisper!" In the courtyard of the castle

six startled geese stopped hunting snails and looked up at the oak room. "What slish is *this*?" exclaimed the Duke, disgusted by the pool of melted gems leering on the table. His monocle fell, and he slashed his sword at silence and at nothing. Something moved across the room, like monkeys and like shadows. The torches on the walls went out, the two clocks stopped, and the room grew colder. There was a smell of old, un-opened rooms and the sound of rabbits screaming. "Come on, you blob of glup," the cold Duke roared. "You may frighten octopi to death, you gibbous spawn of hate and thunder, but not the Duke of Coffin Castle!" He sneered. "Now that my precious gems have turned to thlup, living on, alone and cold, is not my fondest wish! On guard, you musty sofa!" The Todal gleeped. There was a stifled shriek and silence.

When Hark came into the room, holding a lighted lantern above his head, there was no one there. The Duke's sword lay gleaming on the floor, and from the table dripped the jewels of Hagga's laughter, that never last forever, like the jewels of sorrow, but turn again to tears a fortnight after. Hark stepped on something that squutched beneath his foot and flobbed against the wall. He picked it up and held it near the lantern. It was the small black ball stamped with scarlet owls. The last spy of the Duke of Coffin Castle, alone and lonely in the gloomy room, thought he heard, from somewhere far away, the sound of someone laughing.